CLEAN
& LEAN
FAST DIET
COOKBOOK

ZOBIT

Original ISBN 13: 978-1-911147-00-0

COPYRIGHT INFORMATION
Texts: ©2016 Nextquisite Ltd, London

ISBN 978-1-911147-37-4, 978-1-911147-38-1, 978-1-911147-39-8 (Paperback)
Zoblit ltd
Unit A Vulcan House, Vulcan Road, Leicester, LE5 3EB

A catalogue record of this book is available from the British Library

New Paperback Cover Design by Manoj Patil (The Rubixion)
Clean & Lean Fast Diet Cookbook cover design © 2016 Manoj Patil - The Rubixion
Edited by Nextquisite Ltd, London

Printed in the United Kingdom

Disclaimer

BREAKFAST

SNACKS

LUNCH

DINNERS

DESSERTS

INTRODUCTION

WHAT IS CLEAN EATING? IS IT FOR ME?

CLEAN UP YOUR DIET AND TRANSFORM YOUR BODY

The Clean & Lean Fast Diet Cookbook provides 60 delicious recipes that will help you to reach your target weight and transform your body into the healthy, clean and lean version of yourself that you have always wanted to be. If that sounds too good to be true, take a few moments to read this brief introduction.

The first thing to remember is that you **can** achieve your ideal body weight as well as a lean and clean silhouette by following a healthy diet and exercising regularly. Recently it has become fashionable to claim that your body clings to unwanted pounds and packs them back on again as soon as you manage to lose a few. This simply isn't true! Your body yearns to be lean and healthy; it is its natural state. However, to be light and lean, your body first needs to be clean and healthy. It needs to rid itself not just of the unwanted pounds, but also of all the toxins it has accumulated over time.

To achieve your health goals and target weight you must understand that clean eating is not a "diet". It is not about reducing calories or excluding certain foods for a period of time until the unwanted pounds are lost, then returning to your previous style of eating. As many of you who have experienced this "yo-yo" pattern of dieting will already know, that doesn't work at all. The weight really does come right back again as soon as you finish your diet. Which makes perfect sense, because that's how it got there in the first place!

Clean eating means adopting a new way of relating to food, being mindful about its origins and preparing and eating it with care. It also means having a positive view of yourself, your place in the world, and your future. But that sounds complicated when really it isn't. Clean eating means consuming delicious, fresh foods that are as close to their natural state as possible. It's as simple as that.

We suggest that you begin your new lifestyle with an initial period of six weeks during which time you modify your eating habits fairly radically so that your body can detox itself and become accustomed to the basic tenants of this style of eating. Well before the end of the six-week initial period you will begin to experience the healthy glow and renewed vigour that will mark the rest of your life. Depending on your starting weight, you will probably lose quite a few pounds during this first phase and if you stick with it you can expect to a drop a dress or trouser size, if not more. If you are carrying a lot of extra weight you may want to repeat the initial phase after a brief pause, or simply prolong it until you reach your target.

The foods that you eat during this first six-week phase will make up eighty to ninety percent of what you will eat from now on. They include:

Vegetables: Low in calories and brimming with antioxidants, vitamins, minerals and fibre, fresh vegetables will be the mainstay of your diet. Frozen vegetables are convenient and also a healthy choice, so long as they don't contain added salt or include sauces. Canned vegetables can also be good, but check that they don't contain added salt. Some vegetables, such as potatoes, are high in carbs. This doesn't mean you can't eat them, just be aware that they have more calories.

Fruit and Nuts: Fresh fruit and nuts are always a healthy food choice. Just make sure that they are as close to nature as possible. Nuts should not be roasted, toasted or salted. And remember that nuts are high in calories. A daily serving is what will fit easily into the palm of your hand. Fruits should be fresh and preferably organic. But they can also be frozen or canned — just make sure there is no added sugar.

Whole Grains: The key thing is to eat whole grains, not refined. These include brown rice, whole grain bread, oatmeal, bulgur, whole rye, buckwheat, corn and quinoa, to name a few. Exclude all refined grains, including white flour, white bread, regular pasta and white rice. Unless you are sensitive to gluten, there is no need to eliminate it from your diet.

Legumes: This group includes beans, lentils, peas, chickpeas, and soy beans. Rich in dietary fibre, fresh beans, peas and dried lentils don't require soaking and cook quite quickly. Dried beans require soaking overnight and take and hour or two to cook. Replace with frozen or canned beans, but check the labels carefully and don't buy them if they have added sugar or too much sodium. Always rinse canned beans thoroughly before serving as this will wash off a lot of extra salt.

Dairy: If you like dairy food you can include it in your clean-eating diet. Yoghurt is a good choice, but focus on plain unflavoured yoghurt because the flavoured varieties tend to contain a lot of sugar.

Protein: Eggs are a great source of protein and can be eaten daily. Fish and seafood are a superb source of protein and are packed with a range of minerals too. Be sure to include at least two servings a week of fish that are high in omega-3 fatty acids. The best sources are mackerel, lake trout, herrings, sardines, tuna and salmon. Meats of all kinds can be enjoyed, including chicken, turkey, beef, pork and lamb. Stick to unprocessed meats and if you can afford it, always buy sustainably sourced fish and seafood and organic poultry and meats.

Healthy Fats: Olive oil, cold-pressed nut oils and butters, avocados and coconut oil are all good fats and can be included in your clean eating plan.

Herbs and Spices: Use them freely to flavour your food.

Drinks: Water is what your body most needs and you should drink as much of it as your body requires. About 8 large glasses, or two litres a day, is the recommended daily intake. Flavour it with fresh lemon or lime juice. Tea and coffee can also be consumed, but not more than 1–2 cups daily.

The foods that you should eliminate entirely during this first phase are:
Alcohol: Has no nutritional value.
Refined Sugar: Exclude all cakes, desserts, ice cream, biscuits and so on.
Processed Foods: Check labels and exclude anything with artificial additives, flavourings, colourings, or ingredients you don't recognize.

Once the six-week initial phase is over, you can begin your lifetime of clean eating that will be largely based on the foods listed above but will also include treats such as the occasional slice of cake or glass of wine.

THE SIX-WEEK PLAN THAT WILL CHANGE YOUR LIFE

You have seen in the introduction that by adopting a clean eating plan you can improve your general well being and return to a healthy weight. But it is not just by adopting this clean eating plan that you will achieve total wellness. We suggest that you take six weeks to begin a complete overhaul of your diet, exercise and lifestyle choices. We have identified six general wellness areas and we suggest that you focus on one of them each week to restore and improve your health. The areas are healthy eating, staying active, sleeping well, stress management, being connected, and finding direction and passion in your life.

Week One Focus: Clean Eating

We'd like you to start the plan to change your life by really thinking about what you eat and how it affects your health. Even before you start the diet, you might like to try keeping a food journal to see exactly what you eat and when you eat it. You should also go through your kitchen cupboards and throw out foods that are laden with unhealthy refined flour, sugar and additives.

If you are following the diet plan recommended in the body of this book, you will be well on your way to achieving wellness already. But more generally speaking, there are a few basic rules to consider when planning a healthy diet for yourself and your family, irrespective of specific health issues:

• Eat real foods: Vegetables, fruits, whole grains, nuts, cheese, butter, olive oil, fish and meat are all foods that your grandparents would recognise and eat. These are real foods.

• Prepare these real foods yourself: You don't need to be told that readymade supermarket meals and the like will be full of unhealthy additives, such as sugar, trans-fats, preservatives and artificial colourings and flavourings. If you buy fresh real foods and prepare them at home you know exactly what you are eating.

• Eat real foods as close to their natural state as possible: This doesn't necessarily mean they should be eaten raw, but enjoy them cooked simply so that their natural flavours can shine through. Some of the world's best-loved cuisines, such as Italian and Greek, are quite austere and based on high-quality ingredients that are cooked and served as close to nature as possible.

• Eat foods that are locally grown and in season: Foods that have been harvested before they are mature, kept in cool stores then shipped halfway round the world are unlikely to be full of the nutrients you need for optimum health.

• Eat joyfully: Devote time to the preparation of food and take time to enjoy it, preferably in the company of friends and family. Even if you are eating alone, don't gobble it down on the run or while watching TV.

Week Two Focus: Staying Active

This week we'd like you to maintain your healthy eating plan, but also to take time to think about your exercise goals. Regular physical activity brings so many benefits it's difficult to know where to start. Perhaps most importantly, exercise can help manage health conditions and combat disease. It can prevent and control heart disease, stroke, type 2 diabetes, high blood pressure, cholesterol levels, osteoporosis, arthritis and many types of cancer, to name a few.

Exercise can also stop you gaining weight or help maintain weight loss. When you engage in physical activity, you burn calories. The more intense the activity, the more calories you burn. If you don't have time to work out, get more active throughout the day in simple ways, for example, by walking to work or taking the stairs instead of the lift.

Exercise boosts your mood and increases your energy levels. As you exercise more, you will look and feel so much better, which will encourage you to engage in more exercise. It's a virtuous circle. Exercise will also help you to sleep better and to enjoy a more rewarding sex life.

As you can see, starting a fitness programme may be one of the best things you can do for your health. Remember that you don't have to run a marathon, or even join a gym if you don't want to. In fact, when you're designing your personal fitness programme, think carefully about what you like doing and have time for.

Try to make exercise a fun part of your daily routine; that way you are more likely to stick with it. There's no point signing up for an expensive pilates course across town if your work or family commitments will make it difficult to go. If you have a high pressure job, do you really want another fixed "appointment" locked into your already packed schedule? For you, making a date to power walk with a friend once a week, playing tennis with family or friends on the weekends, and some basic yoga or stretching 2–3 days a week at home, might be enough. And think about booking that ski holiday or walking tour as this will encourage you to get in shape before you leave.

Week Three Focus: Sleeping Well
By week three you will begin to notice that your trousers or skirts are looser at the waist and the scales should also show that you have lost a few pounds. The benefits of your healthy eating and exercise plans will be kicking in so keep them up as you head into the third week of your new life. Now is the time to think about how well you sleep. Resting plays a vital role in maintaining good health and getting enough quality sleep will help protect your mental and physical health, as well as improve your quality of life. Sleep helps your brain to work efficiently. While you are sleeping, your brain is preparing for the next day,

forming new pathways to help you learn and remember information.
Sleep allows your mind and body to restore themselves. For example, sleep is involved in healing and repair of your heart and blood vessels and ongoing sleep deficiency is linked to an increased risk of heart disease, stroke, high blood pressure, kidney disease and diabetes. Sleep deficiency has also been linked to depression, suicide and an increased risk of dementia.

There are a number of things you can do to improve the quality of your sleep:
• Establish a sleep routine by going to bed and waking up at the same time each day: This will regulate your body clock, making it easier to fall asleep and stay asleep all night.
• Daily exercise: Vigorous exercise is best, but even light exercise helps. Exercise at any time of day, but not in the 2–3 hours before you go to bed.
• Evaluate your room and bed: Your bedroom should be cool and free from noise and light. Your bed should comfortable and supportive. Have comfortable pillows and make the room attractive and inviting for sleep.
• Avoid alcohol, cigarettes and heavy meals in the evening as these can disrupt sleep.
• Wind down and relax for an hour or two before bedtime: Your body needs time to shift into sleep mode, so spend time doing a calming activity such as reading. Using an electronic device such as a laptop can make it hard to fall asleep, because the particular type of light emanating from the screens of these devices is activating to the brain.

Week Four Focus: Stress Management
This week, in addition to maintaining your healthy eating plan, exercise programme, and sleeping well focus, we'd like you zero in on managing stress and living serenely. When stressed, the body thinks it is under attack and switches to "fight or flight" mode, releasing a mixture of hormones and chemicals such as cortisol and adrenaline to prepare the body for physical action.

This causes a series of reactions, from blood being diverted to muscles to shutting down unnecessary bodily functions such as digestion. Stress is not always a bad thing. Sometimes it can help you focus and react appropriately, but long term stress can cause considerable damage, both physically and mentally.

Stress management is about taking charge of your life and the way you deal with problems. No matter how stressful your life seems, there are steps you can take to relieve the pressure and regain control. Try these solutions:
• Learn to say no and avoid situations and people that stress you out.
• Learn to express your feelings instead of bottling them up inside.
• Be solution-oriented: Think "how can I solve this problem", and go ahead.
• Be willing to compromise.
• Think positive and look at the big picture.
• Keep a sense of proportion and your sense of humour.
• Be willing to forgive.
• Follow a healthy diet, get plenty of sleep and exercise regularly. These are all great ways to reduce stress.

Week Five Focus: Being Connected
By week five many of you will be close to reaching your weight and overall health goals. This will bring a feeling of satisfaction and the desire to move forward with your life. This week, we'd like you to stay focussed on healthy eating, staying active, sleeping well and stress management, and also to take the time to think about how you interact with the world. We all need to feel connected, firstly to ourselves and then to the world around us. Feelings of loneliness and isolation can be devastating to your health and often lead to unhealthy lifestyle choices such as overeating, binge drinking and even addiction, whether it be to drugs, alcohol, sex, gambling or even work.
There are many ways to re-connect with yourself, with others and with nature.
• Meditation: Sign up for a course in mindful meditation and learn how to really

feel your emotions and accept them. Get back in touch with you innermost self.
• Switch off: Ironically, this may be one of the best ways to connect. Set aside an hour, a day or a weekend and deliberately disconnect from your everyday life. Switch off your cell phone, don't compulsively check your texts or email or even watch TV. Be silent. Spend time in peaceful harmony with yourself.
• Be kind to yourself and others. Donate some of your time or money to those less fortunate than yourself. Acts of kindness can be as simple as smiling or greeting strangers or being courteous in everyday situations.
• Find time to connect with nature.

Week Six Focus: Finding Direction & Passion in Life

Congratulations! You have reached the last week of your makeover plan. By now you should be feeling and looking your best. During this final week we would like you to stick with your healthy eating plan, exercise routine, sleeping well focus, stress management and staying connected, but we would also like you to look at your long term goals. You only have this one life, so make the most of it. Take time to ask yourself if you are truly happy in the choices you have made and remember that you can always make changes to your life story. If you feel that your life lacks purpose or meaning, if you are constantly tired and discouraged or challenged by anxiety and feelings of inadequacy, you will not be enjoying good health or total wellness. Take the time to examine your life. Try to explain it to yourself as though you were talking about someone else. Step back and try to get some perspective on it, then decide what you can do to improve things.

Once you have decided on the people, job, places and experiences that are important to you, pursue them all with passion. Is your job all wrong for you? Maybe you would prefer to set up your own small business and experience the satisfaction of being your own boss. Perhaps it is time to retire and dedicate yourself to the things that truly interest you. There are many choices to be made in life. Don't take anything for granted.

BREAKFAST

Your body is dehydrated in the mornings, so start the day with a glass of mineral water and the freshly squeezed juice of half a lemon or lime. The best clean-eating breakfasts are high in protein which will keep you feeling focussed and full of energy right through the morning. Slow-releasing carbs, like those found in high-quality homemade granola, muesli or oatmeal are also good.

PINEAPPLE & KIWI LAYERED SMOOTHIES

Ingredients

1 small fresh pineapple,
peeled, tough core removed,
and chopped
250 ml (1 cup) crushed ice
4 kiwi fruit

Special Tip:

These smoothies have a two-toned look that is very attractive for an early morning treat.

Method:

230 CALORIES

* Place two tall glasses in the freezer to chill.

* Combine the pineapple and ½ cup (120 ml) of the crushed ice in a blender and blend until smooth. Pour into the glasses and replace in the freezer.

* Rinse the blender then chop the kiwi fruit with the remaining ½ cup (120 ml) of crushed ice until smooth.

* Pour the green kiwi mixture carefully in on top of the pineapple mixture to make layered smoothies. Serve.

MELON & KIWI SMOOTHIES

SERVES: 2

Ingredients

300 g (2 cups) cubed rock (cantaloupe) melon
1 small Granny Smith apple, peeled, cored, and chopped
1 kiwi fruit, peeled and chopped

2 tbsp liquid honey
1 tbsp fresh lemon juice
120 ml (½ cup) crushed ice

Special Tip:

Kiwi fruit is rich in vitamin C but also in nutrients that protect the heart by reducing the risk of blood clots that cause heart attacks and stroke and by lowering triglycerides.

Method:

190 CALORIES

* Place two medium glasses in the freezer to chill. Reserve a few cubes of melon to garnish.

* Combine the remaining melon with the apple, kiwi fruit, honey, lemon juice, and ice in a blender and blend until smooth.

* Pour into the chilled glasses. Press the reserved melon cubes onto toothpicks and use them to garnish the glasses. Serve.

GREEN SMOOTHIES

SERVES: 2

Ingredients

1 medium banana
1 medium green eating apple, such as a Granny Smith, cored and chopped
150 g (1 cup) seedless white grapes

250 ml (1 cup) plain Greek yogurt
2 cups (100 g) fresh baby spinach leaves

Special Tip:

These smoothies are packed with vitamin K and a host of other antioxidant nutrients. If possible, always choose organic fruit and vegetables. If you can't get organic produce, rinse it very thoroughly before use.

Method:

264 CALORIES

* Place two tall glasses in the freezer to chill. Reserve a few pieces of fruit to garnish.

* Combine the remaining banana, apple, grapes, yogurt, and spinach in a blender and blend until smooth.

* Pour into the glasses. Press the reserved fruit onto toothpicks and use to garnish the drinks. Serve.

BERRY SMOOTHIES

SERVES: 2

Ingredients

75 g (½ cup) fresh blueberries
75 g (½ cup) fresh raspberries
+ extra to garnish
75 g (½ cup) fresh sliced
strawberries

180 ml (⅔ cup) pomegranate
or cherry juice
250 ml (1 cup) unsweetened
almond milk
2 tbsp honey

Special Tip:

Berries are one of nature's superfoods. Eating berries regularly can help prevent heart disease, ward off cognitive decline, manage blood sugar levels and help lower blood pressure.

Method:

140 CALORIES

* Place two tall glasses in the freezer to chill.

* Combine the blueberries, raspberries, strawberries, pomegranate juice, mango juice, milk, and honey in a blender and blend until smooth.

* Pour into the chilled glasses, garnish with the raspberries, and serve.

HOMEMADE GRANOLA

SERVES: 12

Ingredients

400 g (4 cups) rolled oats
250 g (2 cups) mixed nuts and seeds
70 g (1 cup) unsweetened coconut flakes
120 ml (½ cup) apple juice
120 ml (½ cup) liquid honey

60 ml (¼ cup) coconut oil
1 tbsp vanilla essence (extract)
½ tsp cinnamon
1 tsp sea salt flakes
250 g (2 cups) mixed dried unsweetened fruit

Special Tip:

This granola is based on oats. Oats contain a type of soluble fibre known as beta-glucan which can lower cholesterol. Consuming just 3 grams of oat fibre per day (about one bowl of oatmeal) can lower cholesterol by 8–23 per cent.

Method:

320 CALORIES

* Preheat the oven to 325°F (160°C/gas 3).

* Combine the oats, nuts, seeds, and coconut flakes in a large bowl.

* Combine the apple juice, honey, coconut oil, vanilla, cinnamon, and salt in a medium saucepan. Gently heat until the salt is dissolved and the coconut oil is liquid.

* Pour the apple juice mixture over the oats mixture, tossing to coat.

* Spread the mixture out evenly on a large rimmed baking sheet.

* Bake for 25–35 minutes, until golden. Stir the mixture every 10–15 minutes to make sure it bakes evenly.

* Let the granola cool completely. It will become crunchier as it sits. Stir in the dried fruit when completely cool.

* Serve with yogurt or milk and fresh fruit. Store in an airtight container.

HOMEMADE MUESLI

Ingredients

3 cups (300 g) rolled oats
50 g (½ cup) desiccated (shredded) coconut
3 tbsp pumpkin seeds
3 tbsp sunflower seeds
2 tbsp sesame seeds

60 ml (¼ cup) rapeseed oil
60 ml (¼ cup) liquid honey
60 g (½ cup) golden raisins (sultanas)
60 g (½ cup) dried goji berries

Special Tip:

Packed with healthy fibre and natural sources of energy, this muesli is a great way to start the day.

Method:

220 CALORIES

*   Preheat the oven to 350°F (180°C/ gas 4). Line a large shallow baking pan with parchment paper.

*   Mix the oats, coconut, pumpkin seeds, sunflower seeds, and sesame seeds in a large bowl.

*   Combine the rapeseed oil and honey in a small saucepan over medium-low heat. Bring to a gentle simmer. Drizzle over the oat mixture, mixing well.

*   Spread out evenly in the prepared pan. Bake for 20–25 minutes, stirring occasionally, until crisp and golden.

*   Let cool completely, then stir in the golden raisins and goji berries.

*   Serve with yogurt or milk and fresh fruit. It is very good with unsweetened almond milk.

APPLE, NUT & CINNAMON OATMEAL

SERVES: 4

Ingredients

60 g (½ cup) hazelnuts
3 cups (750 ml) unsweetened almond milk
150 g (1½ cups) rolled oats
1 Granny Smith apple, peeled and chopped
3 tbsp ground flaxseed

½ tsp ground cinnamon
¼ tsp sea salt flakes
½ tsp vanilla essence (extract)
2 tbsp brown sugar
4 tbsp slivered almonds

Special Tip:

You could also use cow's milk to make this oatmeal.

Method:

285 CALORIES

* Preheat the oven to 180°C (350°F/ gas 4).

* Spread the hazelnuts out in a baking pan. Bake for 15 minutes, stirring once.

* Turn the hazelnuts out onto a clean kitchen cloth. Roll up the cloth and rub off the skins. Chop the nuts fairly finely using a large knife.

* Combine the almond milk, oats, apple, flaxseed, cinnamon, and salt in a medium saucepan and bring to the boil over medium heat. Stir in the vanilla.

* Cover, reduce the heat to low, and simmer until thick, about 5 minutes.

* Sprinkle with the hazelnuts, brown sugar, and almonds, and serve hot.

BREAKFAST OATMEAL WITH FRESH FRUIT

SERVES: 2

Ingredients

250 ml (1 cup) unsweetened almond milk
250 ml (1 cup) water
¼ tsp sea salt flakes
1 tsp vanilla essence (extract)

100 g (1 cup) rolled oats
2 tbsp maple syrup, to serve
150 g (1 cup) fresh sliced fruit or berries, to serve

Special Tip:

Plain, steel cut or rolled oats are a great clean eating pantry basic. A steaming bowl of freshly made oatmeal makes a healthy start to the day and will power you through the busiest of mornings.

Method:

175 CALORIES

* Combine the milk and water in a heavy-based saucepan over medium-high heat. Add the salt and vanilla and bring to a boil.

* Pour in the oats, stirring vigorously with a wooden spoon. When the water returns to the boil, decrease the heat to low. Simmer, stirring every few minutes, until the oats are creamy and plump, 10–15 minutes.

* Turn off the heat and cover the pan. Let the oatmeal sit for 5 minutes to fully absorb the liquid.

* Pour into serving dishes and serve hot with maple syrup and fresh fruit of your choice.

ALMOND PANCAKES

SERVES: 4

Ingredients

2 large free-range eggs,
separated
1 cup (120 g) finely ground
almonds (almond meal)
3 tsp sugar
3 tbsp unsalted butter,
softened

¼ tsp sea salt flakes
1 tbsp mild-flavoured
olive oil
60 ml (¼ cup) water

Special Tip:

Not only do almonds help protect against heart disease while supporting cognitive function, they also improve your skin.

Method:

220 CALORIES

* Put the egg whites in a big bowl and the egg yolks in a small bowl.

* Add the almonds, sugar, 1 tablespoon of butter, salt, oil, and water to the bowl with the egg yolks and mix well.

* Beat the egg whites until soft peaks form. Fold the egg whites into the almond mixture as gently as possible.

* Heat 1 tablespoon of the remaining butter in a large frying pan. Drop tablespoons of the batter into the pan and cook until golden brown, 2–3 minutes. Flip and cook the other side.

* Repeat with the remaining butter and batter. Serve warm.

BUCKWHEAT PANCAKES

Ingredients

300 g (2 cups) buckwheat groats
1 tsp chia seeds
75 g (½ cup) rice flour
½ tsp bicarbonate of soda (baking soda)
½ tsp ground cinnamon

1 tbsp maple syrup
+ extra, to serve
750 ml (3 cups) water + extra, as required
2 tbsp coconut oil
300 g (2 cups) fresh mixed berries, to serve

Special Tip:

Despite its name, buckwheat is not a grain, which is ideal if you are watching your gluten intake. Buckwheat is a rich source of protein, dietary fibre, four B vitamins and several minerals, including niacin, magnesium, manganese and phosphorus.

Method:

310 CALORIES

* Grind the buckwheat groats in a food processor to a flour-like consistency. Use a spice grinder to grind the chia seeds into a fine powder.

* Combine the buckwheat, chia powder, rice flour, bicarbonate of soda, and cinnamon in a bowl. Add the maple syrup and enough of water to make a smooth, fairly liquid batter.

* Heat a small frying pan over medium heat. Add 1 teaspoon of coconut oil and melt over the bottom of the pan. Add enough batter to cover the pan in a thin layer. Tilt the pan so that it spreads evenly.

* Cook until golden brown, 2–3 minutes each side. Serve hot, with the berries sprinkled over the top and drizzled with extra maple syrup.

CAULIFLOWER & BACON SCRAMBLED EGGS

SERVES: 4

Ingredients

1 medium head cauliflower, cut or broken into florets
4 large free-range eggs, lightly beaten
4 tbsp freshly grated Parmesan cheese

Sea salt & black pepper
½ cup (60 g) diced pancetta or bacon
2 cloves garlic, minced
2 tbsp olive oil

Special Tip:

When cooking vegetables, remember that steaming results in less loss of nutrients than boiling in a potful of water.

Method:

260 CALORIES

* Steam the cauliflower until just tender, 3–5 minutes.

* Beat the eggs and Parmesan in a large bowl. Season with salt and pepper.

* Sauté the pancetta and garlic in the oil in a large frying pan over medium heat until the garlic turns pale gold. Add the cauliflower and mix well.

* Lower the heat and pour in the egg mixture. Cook, stirring constantly, until the egg is set, 3–4 minutes. Serve hot.

COURGETTE SCRAMBLED EGGS

Ingredients

4 tbsp butter
2 tbsp olive oil
2 cloves garlic, minced
4 medium courgettes (zucchini), diced
4 medium tomatoes, diced

Sea salt & black pepper
8 large free-range eggs, lightly beaten
2 tbsp coarsely chopped basil, to garnish

Special Tip:

Courgettes are low in calories and contain significant levels of potassium to control blood pressure and vitamin C to boost your immune system.

Method:

375 CALORIES

* Heat 2 tablespoons of butter with the oil in a large frying pan over medium heat. Add the garlic and sauté until pale gold, 2–3 minutes.

* Add the courgettes and sauté over medium heat for 3 minutes. Stir in the tomatoes and cook for 5 minutes. Season with salt and pepper.

* Beat the eggs in a large bowl. Melt the remaining 2 tablespoons of butter in a large frying pan over medium heat. Add the eggs and stir constantly until set, 3–4 minutes. Season with salt and pepper.

* Transfer the eggs to serving dishes. Top with the zucchini and tomatoes. Sprinkle with the basil and serve hot.

CRUSHED AVOCADO ON TOAST

SERVES: 4

Ingredients

2 small avocados, peeled, pitted, and chopped
4 large thing slices sourdough or wholemeal (whole-wheat) bread

2 vine tomatoes, sliced
2 tbsp olive oil
Sea salt & black pepper
Fresh basil, to garnish (optional)

Special Tip:

Avocados have been shown to improve overall cardiovascular health. Although high in fat, it is largely of the heart-healthy mono-unsaturated type. Avocados are high in calories, so try not to overindulge!

Method:

355 CALORIES

* Put the avocados in a bowl and crush coarsely with a fork.

* Toast the bread.

* Spread the avocados evenly over the toast. Top each piece with a slice or two of tomato.

* Drizzle with the oil and season with salt and pepper. Garnish with the basil, if liked, and serve warm.

BROCCOLI & PANCETTA SCRAMBLED EGGS

SERVES: 2

Ingredients

1 small head broccoli, cut or broken into florets
4 large free-range eggs, lightly beaten
60 g (½ cup) freshly grated Parmesan cheese

Sea salt & black pepper
60 g (½ cup) diced pancetta or bacon
1 clove garlic, minced
1 tbsp olive oil

Special Tip:

The unique combination of antioxidant, anti-inflammatory, and pro-detox components in broccoli make it a powerful food in terms of cancer prevention. Eating just one serving a day may be enough to help prevent cancer.

Method:

385 CALORIES

* Steam the broccoli until just tender, 3–5 minutes. Set aside.

* Beat the eggs and cheese in a large bowl. Season with salt and pepper.

* Sauté the pancetta and garlic in the oil in a large frying pan over medium heat until the garlic turns pale gold, about 1 minute. Add the broccoli and mix well.

* Pour in the egg mixture. Cook over low heat for about 5 minutes, stirring often, until the eggs form large chunks. Serve hot.

SNACKS

It is important to spread your calorie, carb and protein intake evenly across the day. This will maximise your body's capacity to burn fat and keep your blood sugar levels stable. Some days you may need a healthy snack or two to get you through to your next meal. This could be a handful of nuts, a small cup of Greek yoghurt, some fresh fruit or vegetable sticks or some of the recipes in this chapter.

WATERMELON SLUSHIES

Ingredients

500 g (5 cups) diced
watermelon, well chilled
250 ml (1 cup) coconut water
1 litre (4 cups) crushed ice

1 tbsp liquid honey
Wedges of watermelon,
to serve

Special Tip:

These slushies are a great way to cool down and re-hydrate on hot summer days. The combination of watermelon and coconut water makes them super healthy.

Method:

65 CALORIES

* Prepare the watermelon, cutting a few decorative wedges to garnish the glasses. Place on a plate, cover, and chill until ready to serve.

* Place six serving glasses in the freezer to chill for 5 minutes while you prepare the slushies.

* Combine the watermelon cubes, coconut water, crushed ice, and honey in a blender and chop until smooth.

* Pour into the chilled glasses, garnish with the watermelon wedges, and serve.

PEACH & BANANA SMOOTHIES

SERVES: 2

Ingredients

1 banana
1 cup (250 ml) Greek yoghurt
60 ml (¼ cup) fresh orange juice

2 tbsp wheat germ + extra, to dust
120 ml (½ cup) crushed ice
2 peaches, pitted and sliced

Special Tip:

Serve these smoothies after a work out. Bananas are high in fast-acting carbs which will help restore your body's levels of glycogen and rebuild damaged muscles. Bananas also provide lots of potassium.

Method:

240 CALORIES

* Place two glasses in the freezer to chill. Reserve 2 slices of peach to garnish.

* Combine the banana, yogurt, orange juice, wheat germ, ice, and remaining peaches in a blender and blend until smooth.

* Pour into the glasses and garnish with the slices of peach. Dust with extra wheat germ, and serve.

RED PEPPER DIP

SERVES: 8

Ingredients

250 ml (1 cup) pomegranate juice
60 g (½ cup) walnuts, toasted
½ tsp paprika
½ tsp ground cumin
½ tsp cayenne pepper
1 (500-g/16-oz) jar roasted red peppers, drained and coarsely chopped
1 tsp fresh lemon juice
2 tbsp olive oil
Coarse sea salt
Carrot sticks and raw broccoli florets, to serve

Special Tip:

Pomegranate juice is highly nutritious and packed with antioxidants. You can buy it at well stocked supermarkets and health food stores, or from online suppliers.

Method:

135 CALORIES

* Simmer the pomegranate juice in a medium frying pan over medium-high heat until thick, syrupy, and beginning to brown slightly around the edges, 12–13 minutes. This should leave you with 2–3 tablespoons of syrup.

* Coarsely chop the walnuts in a food processor. Add the paprika, cumin and cayenne and blend until finely chopped.

* Add the bell peppers, lemon juice, and pomegranate syrup and process until the mixture is smooth.

* Gradually add the oil in a thin steady stream and process until combined.

* Transfer the bell pepper dip to a serving bowl, garnish with the carrot stick and broccoli.

HERB & FETA DIP

SERVES: 6

Ingredients

½ cup each fresh mint, parsley, basil and dill
2 cloves garlic, chopped
2 spring onions (scallions), trimmed and sliced
2 tbsp fresh lemon juice
¼ tsp sea salt flakes

60 ml (¼ cup) olive oil
120 g (4 oz) feta cheese
120 ml (½ cup) Greek yoghurt
Freshly ground black pepper
Sliced raw celery, carrots, peppers, to serve

Special Tip:

Vary the herbs according to what you like or have on hand.

Method:

145 CALORIES

* Combine the mint, parsley, basil, dill, garlic, scallions, lemon juice, and salt in a food processor and process until smooth.

* With the motor running, drizzle in the oil until incorporated. Add the feta and process until smooth. Stir in the yoghurt. Season with black pepper.

* Serve the dip immediately with the vegetables.

BABY FRITTATAS

Ingredients

8 large free-range eggs
120 ml (½ cup) milk
½ tsp freshly ground black pepper
¼ tsp sea salt flakes
120 g (4 oz) thinly sliced

prosciutto (parma ham) or bacon, chopped
60 g (½ cup) freshly grated Parmesan cheese
2 tbsp finely chopped parsley

Special Tip:

Packed with essential vitamins and minerals, and a very good source of low-cost protein, eggs are always a healthy choice. Serve a platter of these warm baby frittatas for a casual breakfast or brunch with family and friends.

Method:

132 CALORIES

*   Preheat the oven to 375°F (190°C/ gas 5). Spray two 24-cup mini muffin pans with nonstick spray.

*   Whisk the eggs, milk, pepper, and salt in a large bowl until well blended. Stir in the prosciutto, Parmesan, and parsley. Fill the muffin cups almost to the top with the egg mixture.

*   Bake for 8–10 minutes, until the egg mixture is puffed and set in the centre.

*   Use a rubber spatula to loosen the baby frittatas from the muffin cups and slide them onto a serving platter. Serve warm.

SPINACH & CHEESE TARTS

Ingredients

350 g (7 cups) fresh spinach
6 spring onions (scallions),
finely chopped
4 large free-range eggs,
lightly beaten

400 g (14 oz) cottage cheese
250 g (2 cups) coarsely grated
Cheddar cheese

Special Tip:

*These little tarts make a great after-school snack for hungry children.
They can also be served as an appetizer.*

Method:

200 CALORIES

* Preheat the oven to 325°F (170°C/ gas 3). Lightly grease eight 2-inch (5-cm) tartlet pans.

* Put the spinach in a saucepan with 250 ml (1 cup) of water. Cook over medium heat, stirring occasionally, until tender, 1–2 minutes.

* Drain well, and let cool for a few minutes. Squeeze out the excess moisture with your hands.

* Place in a bowl and stir in the spring onions, eggs, and both cheeses. Divide the mixture evenly among the prepared pans.

* Bake for 45–55 minutes, until the eggs are set. Serve warm.

CHEESE & PEAR WITH MANUKA HONEY

Ingredients

4 tasty ripe eating pears, preferably organic
2 tbsp fresh lemon juice
6 tbsp manuka honey
250 g (8 oz) firm, tasty

cheese, such as pecorino, Parmesan, or sharp, full-flavoured blue cheeses

Special Tip:

Manuka honey is harvested in New Zealand from bees that feed on the flowers of the manuka bush. It has antibacterial properties that can heal a variety of conditions, from sore throats and stomach aches to irritable bowel syndrome.

Method:

220 CALORIES

*   If using organic pears, leave the peel on—they make the dish much tastier, and healthier.

*   Core the pears and cut into wedges. Drizzle with the lemon juice to stop them from turning brown. Drizzle with the honey.

*   Slice the cheese thinly and arrange the pears and cheese on a serving dish. Serve at once.

LENTIL & SPINACH TOASTS

SERVES: 8

Ingredients

250 g (1½ cups) Le Puy lentils
750 ml (3 cups) vegetable
stock
1 granary baguette, sliced
5 tbsp olive oil
1 large onion, coarsely
chopped

Sea salt & black pepper
4 tomatoes, peeled and
coarsely chopped
500 g (1 lb) spinach
2 tbsp balsamic vinegar
2 cloves garlic, peeled

Special Tip:

Small, dark green Le Puy lentils come from France and have a wonderful flavour. They hold their shape and don't become mushy during cooking, making them ideal for salads and snacks like this one.

Method:

285 CALORIES

* Put the lentils in a large saucepan with the stock. Bring to a boil, then simmer on low heat until tender, 25–30 minutes. Drain and set aside.

* Preheat the oven to 180°C (350°F/ gas 4). Spread the bread out on a baking sheet and toast in the oven.

* Heat 1 tablespoon of oil in a medium saucepan over medium heat. Add the onion and sauté until softened, 3–4 minutes. Season with salt.

* Add the tomatoes and lentils and sauté for 2–3 minutes. Add the spinach and cook until wilted, 2–3 minutes.

* Whisk the remaining 4 tablespoons of oil with the balsamic vinegar in a small bowl. Season with salt and pepper.

* Rub the toast all over with the garlic. Arrange the toast on serving dishes and spoon the lentil and spinach mixture over the top. Drizzle with the oil and vinegar mixture and serve.

LUNCH

Most of us have busy days with work or other commitments outside the home that can make it difficult to stay on our clean eating track. To avoid temptation, prepare food ahead of time so that it is ready when you get home, or take it with you to work. The soups in this chapter can all be re-heated in the office microwave, and the salads will be just as tasty if prepared the night before.

BROCCOLI SOUP

SERVES: 4

Ingredients

1 large head broccoli (about 1 kg/2 lb)
2 tbsp olive oil
2 cloves garlic, finely chopped

1 large potato, peeled and diced
1 litre (4 cups) vegetable stock
Sea salt & black pepper

Special Tip:

Broccoli is packed with antioxidants that help fight inflammation and detoxify the body. Regular consumption is believed to help prevent cancer.

Method:

225 CALORIES

* Separate the broccoli into florets. Chop the stalk into small dice and coarsely chop the leaves.

* Heat 1 tablespoon of oil in a large soup pot over medium heat. Add the garlic and sauté until softened, 2–3 minutes. Add all the broccoli, the potato, and vegetable stock. Season with salt and pepper.

* Partially cover the pan and simmer over low heat until the broccoli is very tender, about 10 minutes.

* Chop the soup with a handheld blender until smooth. Ladle into serving bowls.

* Chop the soup with a handheld blender until smooth. Drizzle with the remaining oil and serve hot.

MINTY PEA SOUP

Ingredients

2 tbsp olive oil
6 spring onions (scallions), sliced
2 cloves garlic, chopped
2 slices bacon, chopped
750 ml (3 cups) vegetable stock

500 g (1 lb) peas
250 g (5 cups) baby spinach
2 tbsp chopped mint
Sea salt & black pepper
6 tbsp Greek yoghurt, to serve

Special Tip:

For a delicious summer lunch or light meal, cook the soup and blend until smooth, then transfer to a bowl, cover, and chill in the coldest part of the refrigerator for at least four hours. Serve cold.

Method:

230 CALORIES

* Heat the oil in a soup pot over medium heat. Add the spring onions, garlic, and bacon and sauté until the spring onions are softened, 3–4 minutes.

* Pour in the vegetable stock and bring to a boil. Add the peas, bring back to a boil, then reduce to a gentle simmer. Stir in the spinach and mint. Simmer until the peas are tender, about 5 minutes.

* Chop the soup with a handheld blender until smooth. Season with salt and pepper. Return to the stove top and gently reheat.

* Ladle the soup into six soup bowls. Swirl a tablespoon of yoghurt into each bowl, and serve hot.

RED LENTIL SOUP

Ingredients

1 tbsp olive oil
1 small onion, minced
2 cloves garlic, finely chopped
4 tbsp chopped dried mango
200 g (1 cup) red lentils
2 potatoes, peeled and diced
3 cups (750 ml) chicken stock

1 (400-g/14-oz) can tomatoes
¼ tsp each ground cumin,
chile powder, sweet paprika
and dried thyme
Sea salt & black pepper
2 tbsp fresh lemon juice

Special Tip:

Like other legumes, lentils are packed with heart-healthy dietary fibre. The good thing is that they don't require soaking and can be cooked in under 30 minutes.

Method:

480 CALORIES

*   Heat the oil in a medium soup pot over low heat. Add the onion, garlic, and mango and sauté until softened, about 5 minutes.

*   Add the lentils, potatoes and chicken stock. Bring to the boil, then simmer for 20 minutes.

*   Stir in the tomatoes, cumin, chile powder, paprika, and thyme. Season with salt and pepper. Simmer until the lentils are tender, about 10 minutes. Stir in the lemon juice.

*   Remove from the heat and blend with a handheld blender until smooth. Return to the heat for 2–3 minutes.

*   Garnish with a little extra dried thyme and serve hot with the toast.

THAI CHICKEN SOUP

SERVES: 4

Ingredients

6 cups (1.5 litres) chicken stock
2 tsp finely grated fresh ginger
2 spring onions (scallions), finely chopped
1 stalk lemongrass, cut in short lengths

100 g (½ cup) jasmine rice
250 g (8 oz) minced (ground) chicken
2 tbsp Thai fish sauce
Fresh cilantro (coriander), to garnish
1 red chili, minced

Special Tip:

This delicious soup is big on taste but light on calories.

Method:

160 CALORIES

* Bring the chicken stock to the boil in a medium soup pot over medium heat. Add the ginger, spring onions, lemongrass and rice.

* Return to the boil, lower the heat, and simmer until the rice is very soft, 25–30 minutes. Remove and discard the lemongrass.

* Break off pieces of chicken and shape into balls about the size of small marbles. Add to the soup and simmer until cooked, 5–8 minutes.

* Stir in the fish sauce, and garnish with the cilantro and chili. Serve hot.

ITALIAN SPRING VEGETABLE SALAD

SERVES: 4

Ingredients

500 g (1 lb) new potatoes
150 g (1 cup) broad (fava) beans
1 bunch tender asparagus
150 g (1 cup) peas
100 g (3½ oz) prosciutto, thinly sliced

200 g (4 cups) mixed salad
100 g (3½ oz) Parmesan
1 cup (50 g) watercress
5 tbsp olive oil
2 tbsp cider vinegar
Pinch of sugar
Sea salt & black pepper

Special Tip:

Steamed new potatoes are a good source of dietary fibre, vitamin B6, potassium and a range of other nutrients. They can help to lower blood pressure and promote cardiovascular health.

Method:

440 CALORIES

* Steam the potatoes until tender, 10–15 minutes. Set aside.

* Steam the fava beans and asparagus until just tender, 2–3 minutes, depending on size.

* Blanch the peas in lightly salted boiling water for 1–2 minutes. Drain well.

* Toss the asparagus, beans, peas, potatoes, and prosciutto together in a salad bowl.

* For the dressing, coarsely grate ½ cup of the Parmesan and combine with the watercress, oil, cider vinegar, and sugar in a food processor. Chop until smooth. Season with salt and pepper.

* Toss the mixed salad leaves with half the dressing and arrange on four serving plates. Pile the vegetable mixture on top and drizzle with the remaining dressing.

* Top with the remaining Parmesan in shavings, and serve.

BEETROOT & BEANS WITH GOAT'S CHEESE

SERVES: 4

Ingredients

500 g (1 lb) beetroot (beets)
250 g (8 oz) broad (fava) beans
120 g (4 oz) goat's cheese, crumbled
Sea salt & black pepper
1 lemon, halved

5 scallions (spring onions), thinly sliced
2 tbsp chopped fresh tarragon
100 g (2 cups) salad greens
4 tbsp olive oil + extra
1 tbsp balsamic vinegar
Pinch of sugar

Special Tip:

Beetroot are a unique source of phytonutrients called betalains, which have strong antioxidant, anti-inflammatory and detoxification health benefits.

Method:

350 CALORIES

* Trim the beets, then stem until just tender, 30–45 minutes, depending on size. Drain under cold running water, and rub off the skins while still warm.

* Steam the beans until tender, 2–4 minutes, depending on size.

* Season the goat cheese with salt, pepper, and a squeeze of lemon juice.

* For the dressing, whisk the oil, vinegar, sugar, and a pinch of salt in a bowl.

* Cut the beets into thin wedges. Transfer to a bowl and toss with the dressing.

* Add the beans, scallions, and tarragon, and toss again. Arrange the salad on a serving dish and top with the beetroot mixture. Drizzle with a little extra oil.

* Top with the goat's cheese, and serve.

AVOCADO SALAD WITH CROUTONS

SERVES: 4

Ingredients

6 tbsp olive oil
2 thick slices firm-textured
bread, cubed
1 tbsp dried oregano
4 cups (200 g) mixed rocket
(arugula), spinach and
watercress leaves

2 avocados, peeled, pitted
and diced
1 tbsp white wine vinegar
1 tsp Dijon mustard
Sea salt & black pepper

Special Tip:

Avocados are very nutritious and contain a wide variety of nutrients, including 20 different vitamins and minerals.

Method:

390 CALORIES

*   Heat 2 tablespoons of the oil in a medium frying pan over medium heat. Add the bread and dried oregano and sauté until golden brown, about 5 minutes.

*   Combine the mixed salad greens and avocados in a salad bowl and toss gently.

*   To prepare the dressing, whisk the remaining 4 tablespoons of oil with the vinegar and mustard in a small bowl. Season with salt and pepper.

*   Drizzle the salad with the dressing and toss gently. Sprinkle the croutons over the top, and serve.

ROASTED BUTTERNUT SQUASH SALAD

Ingredients

2 kg (4 lb) butternut squash, peeled and cubed
6 tbsp olive oil
Sea salt & black pepper
200 g (1 cup) Le Puy lentils
4 cups (200 g) rocket (arugula)

1 tsp sesame seeds
6 spring onions (scallions), sliced
2 tbsp balsamic vinegar
1 red chili, chopped
1 garlic clove, minced
1 tsp honey

Special Tip:

Butternut squash is packed with dietary fibre, vitamins and other nutrients. Eating it regularly can help lower blood pressure, regulate blood sugar and boost your immune function, among other things.

Method:

340 CALORIES

* Preheat the oven to 200°C (400°F/ gas 6).

* Put the squash on a baking sheet, drizzle with the oil and season with salt and pepper. Roast for 20–30 minutes, until tender.

* Cook the lentils in salted boiling water until tender, 15–20 minutes. Drain well and let cool a little in the colander.

* For the dressing, whisk the oil, vinegar, chili, garlic, and honey in a small bowl.

* Put the rocket in a shallow serving bowl and arrange the lentils and squash on top.

* Drizzle with the dressing, top with the sesame seeds and scallions, and serve.

LENTIL SALAD

SERVES: 6

Ingredients

2 cups (400 g) le Puy lentils
½ tsp cumin seeds
1 tsp sea salt flakes
4 spring onions (scallions), sliced
1 cup (50 g) chopped parsley
12 cherry tomatoes, halved

150 g (5 oz) feta, cubed
120 ml (½ cup) olive oil
2 tbsp fresh lemon juice
¼ tsp freshly ground black pepper

Special Tip:

Lentils are a very healthy food. They are an excellent source of dietary fibre, which helps protect against heart disease and many cancers. Lentils also contain protein and useful amounts of folate and magnesium.

Method:

320 CALORIES

* Put the lentils in a medium pan with 6 cups (1.5 litres) of cold water, the cumin, and salt and bring to the boil over medium-high heat. Cover and simmer gently until tender, 15–20 minutes.

* Drain the lentils well and transfer to a large salad bowl. Let cool for a few minutes while you prepare the other ingredients.

* Add the scallions, parsley, tomatoes, and feta cheese to the lentils and toss gently.

* For the dressing, whisk the oil, lemon juice, salt, and pepper in a small bowl.

* Drizzle the dressing over the salad, and serve.

CANNELLINI SALAD WITH TOMATO PESTO

Ingredients

12 sun-dried tomatoes
90 ml (⅓ cup) rice vinegar
1 tbsp olive oil
2 tsp molasses
1 tbsp soy sauce
200 g (4 cups) rocket (arugula)
1 bunch watercress

8 plum tomatoes, diced
6 spring onions (scallions)
100 g (1 cup) black olives
1 (400-g/14-oz) can cannellini beans, rinsed & drained
Sea salt & black pepper
60 g (½ cup) chopped walnuts

Special Tip:

Cannellini beans are supercharged with antioxidants and regular consumption will also help to lower blood sugar levels and prevent bowel cancer.

Method:

355 CALORIES

*   Put the sun-dried tomatoes in a medium bowl and add 1 cup (250 ml) of boiling water. Let stand until the water cools, about 30 minutes.

*   Drain the tomatoes and chop in a food processor with the rice vinegar, oil, molasses, and soy sauce until smooth.

*   Combine the arugula and watercress in a large salad bowl and add the tomatoes, scallions, olives, and cannellini beans. Season with salt and pepper and toss gently.

*   Drizzle the salad with the tomato pesto and toss well. Sprinkle with the walnuts, and serve.

WARM GOAT'S CHEESE SALAD

SERVES: 4

Ingredients

2 tbsp white wine vinegar
½ tsp sea salt flakes
Pinch of sugar
Freshly ground black pepper
5 tbsp olive oil
1 shallot, thinly sliced
2 tbsp honey

4 soft goat cheese rounds,
about 40 g (1½ oz) each
1 tbsp chopped fresh thyme
4 heads red radicchio, sliced
12 cherry tomatoes, halved
½ cup (50 g) sunflower seeds

Special Tip:

We're sure you know that goat's cheese has a unique and delicious flavour, but did you also know that it contains about twice as much protein and almost one third less calories than cheese made from cow's milk?

Method:

420 CALORIES

* To prepare the dressing, whisk the vinegar, salt, sugar, and a good grinding of pepper in a small bowl. Whisk in the oil until well blended.

* Stir the shallot into the dressing and adjust the seasoning.

* Drizzle the honey over the cheese and sprinkle with the thyme.

* Preheat the overhead grill (broiler) in the oven to medium-high.

* Put the cheese underneath for a few minutes, until the tops turn light golden.

* Arrange the radicchio and tomatoes and top with the cheese.

* Drizzle with the dressing and sprinkle with the sunflower seeds. Serve warm.

BACON & EGG SALAD

SERVES: 6

Ingredients

6 thin slices sourdough bread
3 cloves garlic
6 cups (300 g) mixed salad greens
1 tbsp snipped fresh chives
1 red pepper, thinly sliced
6 large thick slices bacon

1 tbsp vinegar
6 large free-range eggs
2 tbsp red wine vinegar
1 tbsp balsamic vinegar
Sea salt & black pepper
1 tsp Dijon mustard
6 tbsp olive oil

Special Tip:

You could also serve this hearty dish for breakfast or brunch.

Method:

410 CALORIES

* Toast the bread. Rub the slices with 2 of the garlic cloves, then cut the bread into small squares.

* Combine the salad greens, chives, bell pepper, and toasted squares of bread in a large bowl.

* Dry-fry the bacon in a frying pan until crisp and golden, about 5 minutes. Drain on paper towels. Cut into thin strips.

* Fill a large shallow pan with water, and bring to a boil. Add the vinegar. Break the eggs into a cup one at a time,

then pour into the pan. Turn off the heat under the pan and cover tightly with the pan lid. Set aside for 4 minutes.

* Place a clean cloth next to the pan. Use a slotted spoon to scoop out the eggs and place on the cloth.

* To prepare the dressing, whisk both vinegars with the mustard and oil in a small bowl. season with salt and pepper.

* Drizzle over the salad and divide among six serving plates. Top each one with an egg and some bacon. Serve.

ASPARAGUS SOUFFLÉS

SERVES: 6

Ingredients

3 tbsp butter
2 tbsp plain (all-purpose) flour
1 cup (250 ml) milk
Sea salt flakes
Semolina or fine dry bread crumbs, to sprinkle

12 stalks asparagus, trimmed
3 tbsp freshly grated Parmesan cheese
3 large free-range eggs, separated + 1 large egg yolk
⅛ tsp freshly grated nutmeg

Special Tip: *Fresh, locally grown asparagus is an excellent source of vitamin K and folate and a good source of many other nutrients. Its nutritional value falls sharply during storage so it should be eaten as soon as possible after picking.*

Method:

145 CALORIES

*   Melt 2 tablespoons of the butter in a small saucepan over medium-low heat. Add the flour and cook and stir for 2 minutes. Gradually whisk in the milk and a pinch of salt. Bring to a gentle boil, stirring constantly.

*   Decrease the heat to low and simmer until the sauce thickens. Set aside.

*   Preheat the oven to 170°C (325°F/gas 3). Butter six small soufflé dishes and sprinkle with semolina or bread crumbs.

*   Steam the asparagus until just tender, 3–4 minutes (depending on the thickness of the stalks). Chop coarsely.

*   Stir the asparagus, Parmesan, egg yolks, and nutmeg into the cream sauce.

*   Beat the egg whites and salt in a bowl until stiff. Fold into the asparagus mixture. Spoon into the soufflé dishes.

*   Bake for 20–25 minutes, until risen and golden. Serve immediately.

CHERRY TOMATO CLAFOUTIS

SERVES: 4

Ingredients

500 g (1 lb) cherry tomatoes, halved
50 g (1 cup) rocket (arugula) + extra leaves, to garnish
Sea salt & black pepper
2 tbsp plain (all-purpose) flour

4 large free-range eggs
90 ml (⅓ cup) milk
180 ml (¾ cup) crème fraîche
60 g (½ cup) freshly grated Parmesan cheese

Special Tip:

These clafoutis make an attractive lunch dish, but you can serve them any time of the day, from breakfast until supper time.

Method:

320 CALORIES

* Preheat the oven to 200°C (400°F/ gas 6). Oil four 6-inch (15-cm) individual ovenproof dishes.

* Arrange the tomatoes and arugula in the prepared dishes and season with salt and pepper.

* Whisk the flour, eggs, milk, crème fraîche, and half the Parmesan in a bowl until smooth. Pour the mixture over the tomatoes and arugula. Sprinkle with the remaining Parmesan.

* Bake for 15 minutes, until set and golden brown on top. Garnish with the extra arugula and serve hot.

MOZZARELLA & ZUCCHINI FRITTATA

SERVES: 4

Ingredients

6 large free-range eggs
180 g (6 oz) fresh mozzarella
cheese, diced
1 tbsp finely chopped mint
2 tbsp finely chopped basil

Sea salt & black pepper
4 tbsp butter
4 courgettes (zucchini), thinly
sliced

Special Tip:

This is a hearty dish that will leave you feeling full and satisfied throughout the afternoon.

Method:

390 CALORIES

* Whisk the eggs in a large bowl. Stir in the mozzarella, mint, and basil. Season with salt and pepper.

* Melt the butter in a large frying pan over medium-high heat. Add the courgettes and sauté until lightly browned, about 5 minutes.

* Pour in the egg mixture and simmer on medium-low heat until the egg is set and cooked through, 7–10 minutes. Serve hot.

SUMMER VEGGIE & HALLOUMI KEBABS

Ingredients

400 g (14 oz) halloumi cheese
2 large red peppers
(capsicums), seeded
1 green or yellow pepper,
(capsicum), seeded
2 medium courgettes
(zucchini), trimmed

1 large red onion, peeled
12 cherry tomatoes
4 tbsp olive oil
2 tbsp chopped rosemary
1 tbsp chopped mint
2 lemons, cut into wedges

Special Tip:

These skewers are delicious in the summer months when peppers and courgettes are at their succulent best.

Method:

325 CALORIES

* Cut the halloumi, peppers, and courgettes into 4-cm (1½-inch) cubes and chunks. Cut the onion into wedges and keep the cherry tomatoes whole.

* Mix the oil with the rosemary and mint in a bowl, and toss the cheese and vegetables in it.

* Thread the onion, tomatoes, halloumi, courgettes, and bell peppers onto skewers, alternating them piece by piece.

* Preheat an overhead grill (broiler) or barbecue on medium-high heat.

* Grill the skewers until the cheese and vegetables are lightly blackened at the edges and blistering, 5–8 minutes on each side.

* Drizzle with lemon juice, and serve hot.

PRAWN & SCALLOP SALAD

SERVES: 2

Ingredients

16 large prawns (shrimp), heads removed
3 tbsp olive oil
10 large scallops, shucked
1 clove garlic, peeled and

lightly crushed
4 cups (150 g) rocket (arugula) leaves
12 cherry tomatoes, quartered
Sea salt & black pepper

Special Tip:

Prawns are an excellent source of protein, a good source of omega-3 fatty acids and a great way to get iron, zinc and vitamin E into your diet. They are also low in saturated fat.

Method:

250 CALORIES

* Cook the prawns in a medium pot of salted boiling water until pink, 2–3 minutes. Drain and let cool. Remove the shells and devein.

* Heat 1 tablespoon of the oil in a medium saucepan over medium heat. Add the scallops and garlic and cook until opaque, 2–3 minutes.

* Divide the arugula among serving dishes and top with the prawns, scallops, and tomatoes.

* Season with salt and pepper and drizzle with the remaining 2 tablespoons of oil. Serve warm.

SEAFOOD SALAD WITH GRAPEFRUIT

Ingredients

16 large prawns (shrimp),
heads removed
16 large clams, in shell
1 large grapefruit
2 cups (100 g) rocket

(arugula) leaves
8 button mushrooms,
thinly sliced
3 tbsp olive oil
Sea salt & black pepper

Special Tip:

Clams are a high protein seafood with an above average amount of healthful minerals such as selenium, zinc, iron and magnesium as well as B vitamins such as niacin.

Method:

290 CALORIES

* Cook the prawns in a medium pot of salted boiling water until pink, 2–3 minutes. Drain and let cool. Remove the shells and devein.

* Cook the clams in a medium saucepan over high heat until open, 5–10 minutes. Discard any that do not open. Remove the clams from their shells.

* Use a sharp knife to peel the grapefruit. Cut into segments, collecting the juice in a small bowl.

* Divide the arugula among serving bowls. Top with the mushrooms, grapefruit, prawns, and clams.

* Add the oil to the bowl with the grapefruit juice. Season with salt and pepper and whisk to combine. Drizzle over the salads and serve.

SPICY CHICKEN & CORN SALAD

SERVES: 4

Ingredients

3 cobs (ears) corn, with husks
3 tbsp butter, softened
2 tbsp chili paste
1 organic lemon, zest & juice
2 tbsp chopped fresh parsley
Sea salt & black pepper
2 boneless skinless chicken

breasts
3 tbsp olive oil
Pinch of cayenne pepper
1 red pepper, sliced
1 avocado, pitted and sliced
4 cups (200 g) salad leaves

Special Tip:

This salad is a real treat. Serve it during the late summer months when locally-grown corn is at its best.

Method:

460 CALORIES

* Peel back the husks on the corn, leaving the leaves attached at the base. Blend the butter, chili, lemon zest, and parsley in a small bowl. Season with salt and pepper. Smear over the corn, pull the leaves back up. Tie with kitchen string.

* Preheat a grill pan to hot. Grill the corn cobs, turning often, until blackened and tender, 15–20 minutes. Set aside.

* Flatten the chicken breasts lightly with a meat tenderizer. Brush with 1 tablespoon of oil, season with salt, black pepper,

and cayenne pepper, then grill until cooked through, about 5 minutes on each side. Set aside.

* Toss the pepper, avocado, and salad in a bowl. Whisk the remaining oil with the lemon juice, salt, and pepper. Drizzle over the salad, tossing gently.

* Slice the chicken into strips and add to the salad. Remove the string and husks from the corn and use a sharp knife to strip off the kernels. Add to the salad. Toss well and serve warm.

CHICKEN SALAD WITH FRESH FRUIT

SERVES: 4

Ingredients

500 g (4 cups) cooked chicken, cubed (leftover roast chicken or 2 grilled or poached chicken breasts)
4 stalks celery, sliced
150 g (1 cup) seedless red or white grapes, sliced

2 fresh peaches, peeled and cubed
120 ml (½ cup) Greek yoghurt
120 ml (½ cup) sour cream
Sea salt & black pepper
Fresh parsley, to garnish

Special Tip:

This is a great way to use up leftover chicken. Alternatively, you can quickly poach or grill two chicken breasts and prepare the salad with them.

Method:

340 CALORIES

*   Combine the chicken, celery, grapes, and peaches in a large bowl and toss gently.

*   Whisk the yoghurt and sour cream in a small bowl then drizzle over the salad. Season with salt and pepper.

*   Chill in the refrigerator for 30 minutes. Garnish with the parsley and serve.

CHICKEN & MANGO SALAD

SERVES: 4

Ingredients

6 shallots
2 small red chilies
1 tbsp grated ginger
1 unwaxed lime, grated
1 tbsp sunflower oil
Sea salt & black pepper
2 chicken breasts, with skin

1 apple, cut into matchsticks
½ mango, cut into matchsticks
1 small bunch mint
3 scallions (spring onions)
2 tbsp coriander (cilantro)
½ tsp Thai fish sauce
¼ tsp sugar

Special Tip:

This salad is rich in exotic Thai flavours.

Method:

300 CALORIES

* Finely chop the shallots in a food processor. Add one chili, half the ginger, and the lime zest. Chop to a paste. Transfer to a frying pan with the oil, season, and sauté until fragrant, 1–2 minutes. Set aside.

* Preheat the oven to 200°C (400°F/gas 6). Cut the skin from the chicken along one side. Stuff with the shallot mixture.

* Place in a roasting pan and roast for 15–20 minutes, until golden and cooked. Let cool, then tear into bite-size pieces.

* Toss the apple, mango, mint, scallions, and half the cilantro in a bowl. Mix in the fish sauce, sugar, remaining ginger, and lime juice, and set aside.

* Put the roasting pan on the stove top. Spoon off any excess fat, then gently heat, scraping up the juices. Chop the remaining cilantro. Finely chop the remaining chili. Stir into the sauce

* Toss the salad with the chicken and dressing, and serve warm.

HONEY & MUSTARD CHICKEN SALAD

SERVES: 4

Ingredients

60 ml (¼ cup) liquid honey
2 tbsp wholegrain mustard
Sea salt & black pepper
2 boneless skinless chicken breasts, halved

4 cups (200 g) mixed salad
20 cherry tomatoes, halved
90 ml (⅓ cup) olive oil
2 tbsp balsamic vinegar

Special Tip:

You can whip this delicious, healthy salad up in just a few minutes. It is ideal for a quick family meal or for casual entertaining.

Method:

420 CALORIES

*   Whisk the honey and mustard in a small bowl. Season with salt and pepper. Brush all over the chicken breasts.

*   Preheat a grill pan (griddle), the overhead grill (broiler) in the oven, or a barbecue grill on medium-high heat.

*   Grill the chicken until cooked through and golden, 5–10 minutes, depending on the cooking method.

*   Let the chicken cool for 5 minutes, then slice.

*   Combine the salad greens and cherry tomatoes in a bowl. Toss well.

*   Divide equally among four serving plates. Top each portion with a quarter of the chicken.

*   To prepare the dressing, whisk the oil and balsamic vinegar in a small bowl. Season with salt and pepper. Drizzle over the salads, and serve.

CHICKEN & ORANGE COUSCOUS SALAD

SERVES: 4

Ingredients

2 boneless skinless chicken breasts, cut into bite-size pieces
4 tbsp olive oil
Sea salt & black pepper
1 cup (180 g) couscous
8 tbsp fresh lemon juice

4 oranges, 2 juiced and 2 into chunks
1 tsp ground cumin
1 clove garlic, minced
1 cup each chopped basil and coriander (cilantro)
4 cups (200 g) watercress

Special Tip:

Nutritious and easy to prepare, this tasty salad makes a great family lunch.

Method:

450 CALORIES

*   Preheat a grill pan (griddle), the overhead grill (broiler) in the oven, or a barbecue grill on medium-high heat.

*   Drizzle the chicken with 2 tablespoons of the oil and season with salt and pepper. Grill the until cooked through and brown on the outside, 10–15 minutes.

*   Put the couscous in a bowl and pour in enough boiling water to cover by about 2.5 cm (1 inch). Set aside to soak for 15 minutes, until the couscous has absorbed the liquid

*   Whisk the lemon and orange juice with the cumin, garlic, and remaining 2 tablespoons of oil. Season with salt and pepper. Pour over the couscous and let soak for 10 minutes.

*   Add the orange chunks, chicken, basil, cilantro, and watercress to the couscous in the bowl, mix well, and serve.

SPICY CHICKEN & APPLE SALAD

Ingredients

2 stalks lemongrass, chopped
2 fresh red chilies, chopped
3 cloves garlic, chopped
1 (2.5-cm(1-inch) piece ginger
2 tbsp sesame oil
2 chicken breasts
1 tsp chili powder

2 tbsp Thai fish sauce
1 red onion, chopped
2 romaine (cos) lettuces
1 cucumber, sliced
1 cup (50 g) bean sprouts
2 stalks celery, sliced
1 green apple, diced

Special Tip:

Use boneless, skinless chicken breasts in this recipe. The salad will be even more delicious if you drizzle it with 3 tablespoons of fresh lime juice and top with a handful of fresh coriander (cilantro) just before serving.

Method:

260 CALORIES

* Combine the lemongrass, chilies, garlic, and ginger in a food processor and chop finely.

* Heat a wok over high heat and add the oil. Add the lemongrass mixture and stir-fry for 1 minute. Add the chicken and chili powder and stir-fry for 4 minutes.

* Add the fish sauce. Decrease the heat to medium and let the chicken and fish sauce bubble for 5 minutes, stirring often. Add the onion and stir-fry for 1 minute. Remove from the heat.

* Arrange the lettuce, cucumber, bean sprouts, celery, and apple on four serving plates. Top with the chicken mixture. Serve warm.

STEAK & AVOCADO SALAD

Ingredients

4 tbsp olive oil
4 (120-g/4-oz) boned sirloin steaks, trimmed of fat
Sea salt & black pepper
3 tbsp balsamic vinegar
1 tsp Dijon mustard

1 clove garlic, minced
200 g (4 cups) mixed salad
20 cherry tomatoes, halved
1 avocado, peeled, pitted and thickly sliced
1 cup fresh coriander (cilantro)

Special Tip:

Steak is a good source of many different minerals, including iron, phosphorus, zinc and selenium. Buy organic, grass-fed steak if you can afford it.

Method:

500 CALORIES

* Rub 2 tablespoons of oil over the steaks and season with salt and pepper. Preheat a large grill pan (griddle) over medium-high heat.

* Grill the steaks until cooked to your liking, 3–4 minutes each side for medium-rare. Remove from the pan and set aside on a plate while you prepare the other ingredients.

* To prepare the dressing, whisk the remaining 2 tablespoons of oil, vinegar, mustard, garlic, and juices from the steak in a small bowl.

* Slice the steaks thinly against the grain.

* Combine the salad greens, cherry tomatoes, avocado, and coriander in a bowl, tossing to coat.

* Divide the salad evenly among four serving plates. Top with the steak, drizzle with the dressing, and serve warm.

BLUE CHEESE & STRAWBERRY SALAD

SERVES: 4

Ingredients

4 tbsp olive oil
4 tbsp balsamic vinegar
1 tsp Dijon mustard
Sea salt & black pepper
4 large slices bread
1 clove garlic

200 g (4 cups) rocket (arugula)
300 g (2 cups) strawberries, halved
4 large thin slices prosciutto
150 g (5 oz) blue cheese, crumbled

Special Tip:

Serve small bowls of this delicious salad as an appetizer before a more substantial course, or pile it onto plates and serve as a one-dish lunch.

Method:

410 CALORIES

* To prepare the dressing, whisk the oil, balsamic vinegar, and mustard in a small bowl. Season with salt and pepper, whisking to combine.

* Preheat the oven to 200°C (400°F/ gas 6).

* Toast the bread in the oven until crisp and golden brown, about 5 minutes. Let cool a little, then run all over with the garlic. Tear into pieces.

* Combine the arugula and strawberries in a large bowl.

* Add the prosciutto, bread, and crumbled blue cheese. Toss gently to combine.

* Drizzle with the dressing, toss gently, and serve immediately.

DINNER

For many of us dinner is the most important meal of the day. When the work day is over we have time to relax and prepare something delicious to refuel after the being on the go all day and to usher in a restful night's sleep. The best solution is often a portion of high quality protein such as fish or meat along with two or three vegetables and a piece of fresh fruit to finish.

CHICKPEA BURGERS WITH SLAW

SERVES: 4

Ingredients

½ small green cabbage
3 carrots, coarsely grated
1 apple, coarsely grated
60 g (½ cup) sultanas
3 tbsp coriander (cilantro)
1 tsp ground cumin
4 tbsp olive oil

2 tbsp fresh lime juice
Sea salt & black pepper
2 (400-g/14-oz) cans
chickpeas, drained and rinsed
4 spring onions (scallions)
75 g (½ cup) bread crumbs
1 large free-range egg

Special Tip:

This delicious healthy meal is rich in dietary fibre that will help lower blood glucose levels as well as protecting against heart disease.

Method:

420 CALORIES

* Shred the cabbage finely and combine in a bowl with the carrots, apple, sultanas, coriander and cumin. Drizzle with the oil and lime juice. Season with salt and pepper. Toss to combine.

* Cover and chill for 2–4 hours to allow flavours to develop.

* Combine the chickpeas, spring onions, bread crumbs, peanuts, cumin, and ginger in a food processor. Season with salt and pepper. Pulse until coarsely chopped. Transfer half the mixture to a

bowl. Add the egg to the food processor and pulse until smooth. Add to the mixture in the bowl, mixing well. Shape the mixture into four even patties.

* Preheat a grill pan (griddle) over high medium-heat. Brush both sides of the patties with oil and cook until crisp and browned, 5–6 minutes on each side.

* Serve hot with the coleslaw.

CARROT & BEAN BURGERS

SERVES: 6

Ingredients

750 g (1½ lb) carrots, grated
1 (400-g/14-oz) can chickpeas, drained and rinsed
1 small onion, chopped
2 tbsp tahini
1 tsp ground cumin
1 large free-range egg

3 tbsp olive oil
75 g (½ cup) fine dry bread crumbs
Finely grated zest of 1 unwaxed lemon
3 tbsp sesame seeds
Sea salt & black pepper

Special Tip:

Carrots are rich in antioxidants, vitamins and dietary fibre. They can help protect against heart disease and cancer and can also improve your eyesight, skin and hair.

Method:

250 CALORIES

*   Chop one-third of the carrots in a food processor with the chickpeas, onion, 2 tablespoons of tahini, cumin, and egg. Scrape into a bowl.

*   Heat 1 tablespoon of oil in a large frying pan over medium heat. Add the remaining carrots and stir until softened, 5–6 minutes.

*   Add to the chickpea paste with the bread crumbs, lemon zest, and sesame seeds. Season and mix well.

*   Divide the mixture into six equal portions. Shape into burgers. Cover and chill until ready to cook.

*   Mix the yogurt with the remaining 1 teaspoon of tahini and lemon juice. Chill until ready to serve.

*   Heat a large frying pan and brush the burgers with the remaining 2 tablespoons of oil. Cook the burgers until golden and crisp, about 5 minutes on each side. Serve warm.

THAI SEAFOOD SALAD

SERVES: 6

Ingredients

2 red chilies, minced
1 tbsp Asian fish sauce
1 tbsp brown sugar
90 ml (⅓ cup) peanut oil
¼ cup minced lemongrass
60 ml (¼ cup) fresh lime juice
350 g (12 oz) whole squid

350 g (12 oz) prawns
(shrimp), shelled
350 g (12 oz) baby octopus
1 mango, cubed
200 g (4 cups) watercress
24 cherry tomatoes, halved
1 cup coriander (cilantro)

Special Tip:

Chilies contain a substance called capsaicin, which gives them their characteristic pungency. Capsaicin is believed to bring many health benefits, including reduction of inflammation in the body and natural pain relief.

Method:

431 CALORIES

*   Whisk the chilies, fish sauce, oil, lemongrass and in a small bowl. Season with salt and pepper. Set aside.

*   Cut each squid open lengthwise, without cutting it in half, so you can open it up and lay it flat. Score it with a knife in a diamond pattern, then cut the body into bite-size squares or rectangles. This will help the squid lay flat while grilling.

*   Combine all the seafood in a bowl with half the dressing and marinate for two hours.

*   Combine the mango, watercress, tomatoes, basil, and cilantro in a large bowl.

*   Preheat a large grill pan (griddle) or chargrill over medium-high heat.

*   Grill the seafood in two or three batches, about 5 minutes each batch. Cool the seafood for a few minutes before mixing it into the salad.

*   Dress with the remaining vinaigrette, season with salt and pepper, and serve.

WARM SALMON & POTATO SALAD

SERVES: 4

Ingredients

500 g (1 lb) new potatoes
1 bunch asparagus
6 tbsp olive oil
3 tbsp fresh lemon juice
1 tsp Dijon mustard
2 red chilies, minced
Sea salt flakes

200 g (4 cups) mixed salad
2 tbsp each chopped fresh
parsley and mint
8 radishes, thinly sliced
4 scallions (spring onions),
sliced
4 wild salmon fillets or steaks

Special Tip:

When serving salmon, try to buy wild salmon rather than farmed. It is much leaner and far more nutritious that farmed salmon.

Method:

440 CALORIES

*   Cut the potatoes in half, if large. Boil in lightly salted water until tender, about 10 minutes. Add the asparagus for the final 3–4 minutes. Drain and let cool.

*   Whisk 6 tablespoons of the oil in a small bowl with the lemon juice, mustard, chilies, and salt. Set aside.

*   Combine the potatoes, asparagus, salad, parsley, mint, radishes, and spring onions in a bowl. Drizzle with half the dressing. Arrange on a serving platter

*   Heat the remaining 2 tablespoons of oil in a large frying pan over medium heat and cook the salmon until tender, 2–3 minutes each side.

*   Break the salmon into chunks with a fork and place on the salad. Drizzle with the remaining dressing and serve warm.

GRILLED ORANGE TUNA WITH FENNEL SALAD

SERVES: 4

Ingredients

2 large ripe unwaxed oranges
1 fennel bulb, thinly sliced
2 stalks celery, thinly sliced
12 cherry tomatoes, halved
1 cup (50 g) black olives
200 g (4 cups) mixed salad
1 tbsp finely chopped chervil

1 tbsp finely chopped fresh dill
4 tbsp olive oil
3 tbsp balsamic vinegar
Sea salt & black pepper
2 tbsp capers, drained
4 tuna fillets, about 150 g
(5 oz) each

Special Tip:

Like salmon, tuna is a very good source of omega-3 fatty acids which have proven benefits for cardiovascular health.

Method:

415 CALORIES

* Preheat an overhead grill (broiler) or grill pan (griddle) on medium high. Cut the zest from the oranges in very fine strips with a sharp knife. Blanch the zest in boiling water for 2 minutes. Drain and set aside.

* Combine the fennel, celery, cherry tomatoes, olives, salad greens, chervil, dill, and orange zest in a bowl. Drizzle with 2 tablespoons of oil and the balsamic vinegar. Season with salt and pepper and toss gently.

* Squeeze the juice from the oranges and season with salt and pepper. Gradually beat in the remaining 2 tablespoons of oil until well blended. Stir in the capers.

* Grill the tuna steaks until just cooked through, 2–3 minutes on each side, depending on their thickness. Do not overcook.

* Arrange the salad on a large serving plate. Put the tuna steaks on top and drizzle with the orange and caper dressing. Serve hot.

GRILLED TUNA WITH YOGHURT

SERVES: 4

Ingredients

120 ml (½ cup) plain Greek yoghurt
2 tbsp mayonnaise
1 tbsp fresh lime juice
2 tbsp grated cucumber
150 g (1 cup) seedless white grapes, chopped

2 tbsp melted butter
4 tbsp fresh lemon juice
4 tuna fillets, about 150 g (5 oz) each
Salad greens, to serve
Cherry tomatoes, to serve

Special Tip:

Tuna is an excellent source of niacin and vitamins B6 and B12, as well as a good source of vitamins B1, B2, choline and a range of minerals, such as phosphorus, potassium, iodine and magnesium.

Method:

360 CALORIES

*   Combine the yogurt, mayonnaise, lime juice, cucumber and grapes in a small bowl and set aside.

*   Stir the butter and lemon juice in a small bowl. Brush over the tuna steaks.

*   Preheat an overhead grill (broiler) or grill pan (griddle) on medium high.

*   Grill the tuna steaks until just cooked through, 2–3 minutes on each side, depending on their thickness. Do not overcook.

*   Transfer the tuna to serving plates. Top with yoghurt and cucumber sauce and garnish with the salad greens and tomatoes. Serve hot.

BAKED COD WITH MARSALA

SERVES: 4

Ingredients

200 g (1 cup) brown rice
4 cod fillets, weighing about
150 g (5 oz) each
Sea salt & black pepper
2 tbsp olive oil
3 tbsp pine nuts
180 ml (¾ cup) dry Marsala

wine
1 tbsp finely chopped parsley
1 tbsp chopped oregano
1 lemon, thinly sliced
200 g (4 cups) salad greens
20 cherry tomatoes, halved

Special Tip:

The Marsala adds a lovely flavour to this dish. Don't worry about the alcohol as it will all burn off during cooking.

Method:

430 CALORIES

* Put the brown rice on to cook in a little lightly salted water. Cover and let simmer until tender.

* Preheat the oven to 180°C (350°F/gas 4).

* Arrange the fish in a single layer in a large baking dish. Season with salt and pepper. Drizzle with the oil and sprinkle

with the pine nuts. Pour the Marsala over the fish. Sprinkle with the parsley and oregano.

* Bake for 15 minutes, until lightly browned and cooked through.

* Garnish the fish with the lemon slices and serve hot with the rice, salad, and tomatoes.

SAUTÉED WHITE FISH WITH TOMATOES

SERVES: 6

Ingredients

3 tbsp olive oil
2 onions, finely chopped
1 kg (2 lb) white fish fillets,
such as John Dory, sea bass,
flounder or cod
500 g (1 lb) cherry tomatoes,
halved

1 cup (50 g) black olives,
pitted and halved
250 ml (1 cup) fish or
vegetable stock
Sea salt & black pepper
Fresh basil leaves, to garnish

Special Tip:

White fish fillets are quick and easy to prepare and they are a very good source of high quality lean protein. Just one 120-g (4-ounce) serving of cod has more than 21 grams of protein.

Method:

270 CALORIES

* Heat the oil in a large frying pan over medium heat. Add the onions and sauté until softened, 3–4 minutes.

* Add the fish and simmer for 2 minutes. Turn the fish over and sauté for 2 minutes more. Remove the fish and set aside.

* Add the cherry tomatoes and olives and simmer for 3 minutes. Pour in half the stock and simmer for 2 minutes.

* Pour in the remaining stock and cook for 5 minutes. Return the fish to the pan and warm through.

* Season with salt and pepper and garnish with the basil. Serve hot with the couscous.

BAKED SALMON WITH HERB CRUST

SERVES: 4

Ingredients

2 slices wholemeal (whole-wheat) bread
50 g (1 cup) fresh parsley
3 tbsp olive oil
Sea salt & black pepper
4 skinless wild salmon fillets, about 150 g (5 oz) each

2 tbsp Dijon mustard
3 tbsp fresh lemon juice
150 g (3 cups) mixed salad greens
1 small red onion, thinly sliced
16 cherry tomatoes, halved

Special Tip:

Salmon is an oily fish and very rich in omega-3 fatty acids. Just 120 g (4 oz) of salmon contain about 2 grams of omega-3 fats, which is more than most adults in the United Kingdom get from food over several days.

Method:

340 CALORIES

* Preheat the oven to 220°C (450°F/ gas 8). Line a baking sheet with aluminium foil.

* Combine the bread, parsley, and 1 tablespoon oil in a food processor. Season with salt and pepper. Chop until coarse crumbs form.

* Place the salmon on the prepared baking sheet. Season with salt and pepper. Spread with the mustard and sprinkle with the bread crumb mixture, pressing it down gently to make it stick to the salmon.

* Bake for 12–14 minutes, until the salmon is cooked through and the herb crust is golden.

* Whisk the lemon juice and remaining 2 tablespoons of oil in a large bowl. Season with salt and pepper. Add the salad greens, onion, and cherry tomatoes, and toss to combine.

* Serve the salmon hot with the salad.

PAN-COOKED SALMON WITH COURGETTES

SERVES: 4

Ingredients

2 large courgettes (zucchini), quartered lengthwise and cut into short lengths
4 tbsp butter
500 g (1 lb) skinless wild salmon fillets, cut into small cubes

20 large white seedless grapes, halved
60 ml (¼ cup) dry white wine
90 ml (⅓ cup) water
Sea salt & black pepper
2 tbsp finely chopped parsley, to garnish

Special Tip:

The omega-3 fatty acids, along with the vitamin D and selenium also found in salmon, bring many health benefits, including protection from heart disease and joint degeneration, and improved cognitive function.

Method:

380 CALORIES

*   Cook the zucchini in a large pot of salted, boiling water until just tender, 3–4 minutes. Drain well.

*   Melt 2 tablespoons of butter in a large frying pan over medium heat. Add the salmon and grapes and sauté until the salmon is cooked through and the grapes are softened, about 5 minutes. Transfer to a serving dish and keep warm.

*   Add the wine and water to the cooking juices in the pan and bring to a boil over high heat. Stir in the remaining 2 tablespoons of butter until melted. Add the zucchini and season with salt and pepper. Sauté on high for 1 minute.

*   Add the zucchini to the salmon and grapes. Garnish with the parsley, and serve hot.

GRILLED CHICKEN WITH FETA & OLIVES

SERVES: 4

Ingredients

2 tbsp plain yoghurt
4 tbsp fresh lemon juice
1 tbsp dried oregano
2 tbsp chopped fresh mint
500 g (1 lb) chicken
tenderloins, trimmed
3 tbsp olive oil

3 cups (150 g) spinach
150 g (5 oz) roasted peppers,
from a jar, sliced
1 cucumber, chopped
1 cup (50 g) snow peas
120 g (4 oz) feta cheese
50 g (½ cup) black olives

Special Tip:

If you can't get snow peas, replace them with watercress, rocket (arugula), or another salad green to your liking.

Method:

350 CALORIES

* Combine the yoghurt, 2 teaspoons of the lemon juice, oregano, and mint in a bowl, mixing well. Add the chicken, turning to coat. Cover and chill in the refrigerator for 30 minutes.

* Preheat a grill pan (griddle), overhead broiler (grill), or barbecue grill on medium heat.

* Remove the chicken from marinade and brush with the oil. Grill or broil until cooked through, 5–10 minutes, depending on the cooking method.

* Combine the spinach, bell pepper, cucumber, snow pea sprouts, feta, and olives in a bowl. Toss to combine.

* Divide the salad among four serving plates. Top each portion with a quarter of the chicken.

* Drizzle with remaining lemon juice and extra oil. Season with salt and pepper, and serve.

GRILLED PORK WITH BERRIES & CHEESE

SERVES: 4

Ingredients

1 red onion, finely chopped
2 tbsp balsamic vinegar
2 tbsp finely chopped parsley
Sea salt & black pepper
4 tbsp olive oil
4 (120-g/4-oz) boneless pork chops

200 g (4 cups) salad greens
100 g (3½ oz) blue cheese, crumbled
1 cup (150 g) fresh raspberries

Special Tip:

These pork chops are quite high in calories but they make a nutritious dish. Be sure to buy farm fresh organic pork, if possible.

Method:

500 CALORIES

* Combine the onion, vinegar, and 1 tablespoon of parsley in a medium bowl. Season with salt and pepper and whisk in the oil.

* Put the pork chops in a shallow dish and season with salt. Add the remaining parsley and 3 tablespoons of the dressing. Turn the pork to coat and set aside to marinate for 15 minutes.

* Preheat a grill pan (griddle) over medium-high heat.

* Grill the pork until cooked through but still moist, 4–5 minutes each side. Set aside to rest for 5 minutes.

* Arrange the salad greens on a large serving platter. Top with the pork and sprinkle with the cheese and raspberries.

* Drizzle with the remaining dressing. Sprinkle with the remaining parsley, and serve warm.

CHICKEN & PESTO BURGERS

SERVES: 4

Ingredients

6 tbsp pesto
500 g (1 lb) minced (ground) chicken breast
Sea salt & black pepper
2 tomatoes, thickly sliced
2 tbsp olive oil

4 wholemeal (whole-wheat) hamburger buns
50 g (1 cup) rocket (arugula)
60 g (½ cup) Parmesan, in flakes

Special Tip:

These burgers look great and taste wonderful. The chicken provides plenty of lean protein while the wholemeal buns provide fibre and vitamins.

Method:

460 CALORIES

*   Combine 2 tablespoons of the pesto with the chicken in a bowl. Mix well and season with salt and pepper. Shape into four even patties.

*   Brush the tomatoes with oil and season with salt and pepper.

*   Preheat a grill pan (griddle) to medium-high. Grill the patties until browned on the outside and cooked through, 4–5 minutes on each side.

*   Add the tomatoes to the grill and cook, flipping once, until lightly charred, 2–3 minutes. Toast the buns face-down on the grill for 2–3 minutes.

*   Cover the bottoms of the buns with rocket and tomato. Drizzle with some pesto, cover with the patties, and top with more pesto and the Parmesan flakes. Serve hot.

GREEK BURGERS

SERVES: 4

Ingredients

400 g (14 oz) minced lamb
1 slice bread
1 large free-range egg, beaten
50 g (½ cup) pitted olives
2 cloves garlic, minced
1 tbsp mint
100 g (3½ oz) feta

1 baby cos lettuce, chopped
2 tomatoes, diced
1 small red onion, thinly sliced
1 tsp Dijon mustard
3 tbsp fresh lemon juice
2 tbsp olive oil
120 g (½ cup) tzatziki

Special Tip:

These tasty burgers make a great family meal. Lamb is a very good source of protein, vitamin A, riboflavin, niacin, vitamin B12, iron, zinc, copper and selenium, amongst other things.

Method:

365 CALORIES

* Chop the lamb, bread crumbs, egg, olives, garlic, mint, salt and pepper in a food processor. Stir in the feta.

* Shape into four even burgers. Cover and chill for 1 hour.

* Combine the lettuce, tomatoes, and onion in a bowl.

* Whisk the mustard, lemon juice, oil, salt, and pepper in a small bowl. Pour over the salad and toss to coat.

* Preheat a grill pan (griddle) on medium-high heat. Grill the burgers until cooked to your liking, 4–5 minutes each side for medium-rare.

* Serve the burgers warm with the salad and tzatziki.

GRILLED LAMB WITH SPRING VEGGIES

SERVES: 4

Ingredients

1 bunch asparagus, trimmed
150 g (1 cup) frozen peas
150 g (1 cup) frozen broad
(fava) beans
1 small bunch fresh mint
4 lamb tenderloins or fillets
Sea salt & black pepper

2 cloves garlic, thinly sliced
12 cherry tomatoes, halved
2 tbsp olive oil
2 tbsp balsamic vinegar
1 small bunch fresh tarragon,
chopped

Special Tip:

For extra flavour and colour, add a handful of baby carrots with their stems still attached to the steamer along with the other vegetables.

Method:

415 CALORIES

* Place a large pan of water over high heat. Cover with a steamer pan and lid and bring to a boil. Add the asparagus, peas, beans, and mint and steam until just tender, about 5 minutes. Transfer to a bowl and let cool a little.

* Heat a large grill pan (griddle) or barbecue on high heat.

* Season the lamb with salt and pepper. Sprinkle with the garlic.

* Cook the lamb to your liking; 3–5 minutes each side for medium-rare.

* Add the tomatoes to the bowl with the veggies and toss gently.

* Whisk the oil, vinegar, tarragon, salt, and pepper in a small bowl.

* Divide the vegetable mixture evenly among four serving plates. Drizzle with half the dressing and toss gently.

* Top with the warm lamb, drizzle with the remaining dressing, and serve warm.

GRILLED LAMB WITH GREEN BEANS

SERVES: 4

Ingredients

2 tbsp chopped rosemary
Sea salt & black pepper
500 g (1 lb) lean lamb steak
500 g (1 lb) green beans
150 g (3 cups) baby spinach
50 g (½ cup) black olives
500 g (1 lb) cherry tomatoes,

halved
4 tbsp sherry vinegar
4 tbsp fresh orange juice
2 tbsp olive oil
1 red onion, finely chopped
1 tsp brown sugar

Special Tip:

If possible, use grass-fed organic lamb in this recipe. The dish will be much healthier and the flavours so much better.

Method:

420 CALORIES

* Combine the rosemary, salt, and pepper in a cup. Rub over the lamb and chill in the refrigerator for 1 hour.

* Cook the green beans in salted boiling water until crunchy-tender, 2–3 minutes. Drain and let cool.

* To prepare the dressing, whisk the vinegar, orange juice, oil, onion, brown sugar, salt, and pepper in a small bowl.

* Preheat a grill pan (griddle) or barbecue on high heat. Cook the lamb to your liking; 3–5 minutes each side for medium-rare.

* Slice the lamb. Drizzle with half the dressing and toss gently.

* Combine the spinach, olives, tomatoes, and green beans in a bowl. Top with the lamb. Drizzle with the remaining dressing, and serve warm.

STEAK & CHICKPEA SALAD

SERVES: 4

Ingredients

2 (400-g/14-oz) cans chickpeas, drained & rinsed
1 red onion, thinly sliced
24 cherry tomatoes, halved
½ cup fresh basil leaves
400 g (14 oz) boned sirloin

steak, fat trimmed
Sea salt & black pepper
1 cup (250 ml) plain Greek yoghurt
3 tbsp chili paste

Special Tip:

You can substitute the chili paste with the same amount of harissa.

Method:

490 CALORIES

* Toss the chickpeas, red onion, tomatoes, and basil in a salad bowl.

* Season the steak generously with salt and pepper.

* Preheat a grill pan (griddle) or barbecue on high heat.

* Grill the steak until cooked to your liking, about 5–10 minutes for medium-rare.

* Whisk the yoghurt with the chili paste in a small bowl.

* Slice the steak and add to the salad bowl. Drizzle with the yogurt mixture, toss gently, and serve.

STEAK SALAD WITH BLUE CHEESE

SERVES: 4

Ingredients

1 tsp Worcestershire sauce
4 tbsp olive oil
400 g (14 oz) boned sirloin
steak, fat trimmed
2 tbsp red wine vinegar
1 tsp Dijon mustard
1 tsp honey

2 cloves garlic, minced
Sea salt & black pepper
1 large red onion, sliced
250 g (5 cups) mixed salad
20 cherry tomatoes, halved
100 g (3½ oz) blue cheese,
crumbled

Special Tip:

Steak and blue cheese go very well together, as this recipe will demonstrate.

Method:

500 CALORIES

* Preheat a large grill pan (griddle) over medium-high heat.

* Combine the Worcestershire sauce and 1 tablespoon of oil in a baking dish just large enough to hold the steak. Add the steak, turning to coat.

* Combine the vinegar, mustard, honey, garlic, salt, and pepper in a bowl. Slowly whisk in the 2 tablespoons of oil.

* Brush the onion with the remaining 1 tablespoon of oil, and grill until tender, 3–4 minutes. Season the steak with salt and pepper and grill with the onion, for 3–4 minutes each side for medium-rare. Let rest for 5 minutes.

* Toss the salad greens and tomatoes with half the dressing and divide among four serving plates.

* Slice the steak, separate the onion into rings, and arrange over the salad. Sprinkle with the cheese, drizzle with the remaining dressing, and serve warm.

CHIMICHURRI BEEF & VEGETABLE KEBABS

SERVES: 4

Ingredients

3 tbsp balsamic vinegar
1 tbsp soy sauce
¼ tsp black pepper
500 g (1 lb) steak, diced
1 courgette (zucchini), sliced
1 onion, cut into 8 wedges
1 red bell pepper, diced

1 yellow bell pepper, diced
½ cup chopped fresh parsley
½ cup chopped oregano
2 cloves garlic, finely chopped
3 tbsp olive oil
1 tbsp fresh lemon juice
¾ tsp coarse sea salt

Special Tip:

Chimichurri is a raw parsley sauce for meat. It comes originally from Argentina and Uruguay, but is now a popular sauce around the world.

Method:

450 CALORIES

* Combine 2 tablespoons of balsamic vinegar, the soy sauce, and pepper in a shallow dish. Add the beef, stirring well to coat.

* Marinate in the refrigerator for 1–24 hours.

* Prepare a medium-hot fire in an outdoor grill or preheat an indoor grill to medium-high heat. Lightly grease with oil.

* Thread the beef onto the skewers, alternating with the zucchini, onion, and bell peppers. Grill until cooked to your liking, 7–8 minutes each side for medium-rare.

* Whisk the parsley, oregano, garlic, oil, remaining balsamic vinegar, lemon juice, and salt in a small bowl.

* Drizzle over the kebabs, and serve hot.

BEEF & SUMMER VEGETABLE KEBABS

SERVES: 4

Ingredients

50 g (¼ cup) brown sugar
120 ml (½ cup) soy sauce
2 cloves garlic, finely chopped
½ tsp ground mustard
½ tsp ground cumin
Sea salt & black pepper
500 g (1 lb) steak, cubed

2 small courgettes (zucchini), trimmed & sliced
2 red peppers (capsicums), cut into small squares
1 red onion, quartered & divided into single layers
3 tbsp olive oil

Special Tip:

These attractive kebabs are packed with protein, vitamins and minerals.

Method:

435 CALORIES

* Whisk the brown sugar, soy sauce, garlic, mustard, cumin, salt and pepper in a medium bowl.

* Pour half the marinade into another bowl. Add the meat to one bowl and the vegetables to the other.

* Cover the bowls with cling film (plastic wrap). Chill for 4 hours, or overnight.

* Prepare a medium-hot fire in an outdoor grill or preheat an indoor grill to medium-high heat. Lightly grease with oil.

* Drain and discard the marinades from the meat and vegetables. Thread alternately onto skewers.

* Grill until cooked to your liking, 10–15 minutes, turning and basting with oil to moisten as required. Serve hot.

TREATS

Eating clean doesn't mean that you can never have a
special treat again. In fact, once you have achieved
your target weight you can allow yourself a healthy
dessert, a square of dark chocolate, or even a slice of
cake. We suggest that you make it a healthy treat,
not something loaded with sugar or unhealthy
trans fats. Try some of our suggestions from the
pages that follow.

RED SMOOTHIES WITH CREAM

SERVES: 2

Ingredients

1 banana
150 g (1 cup) fresh
raspberries + few extra,
to garnish

250 ml (1 cup) unsweetened
cherry juice
250 ml (1 cup) crushed ice
Whipped cream, to serve

Special Tip:

These smoothies make a great dessert, or can be served as a snack at anytime of the day.

Method:

230
CALORIES

* Place two serving glasses in the freezer to chill.

* Combine the banana, raspberries, cherry juice, and ice in a blender and blend until smooth and slushy.

* Pour into the glasses. Top with the cream, if using, and 1–2 whole raspberries

FRESH FRUIT GAZPACHO

SERVES: 4

Ingredients

500 g (5 cups) fresh chilled watermelon cubes
120 ml (½ cup) fresh orange juice
2 peaches, coarsely chopped
150 g (1 cup) large strawberries, chopped

2 tbsp fresh lemon or lime juice
Handful fresh basil leaves, torn
250 ml (1 cup) crushed ice

Special Tip:

Very low in calories, watermelon is an excellent source of vitamin A and lycopene. The anti-inflammatory properties of lycopene are believed to lower the risk of heart disease and several common cancers.

Method:

100 CALORIES

*   Blend the watermelon in a food processor or blender until liquified. Transfer to a medium bowl.

*   Strain the orange juice and add to the bowl with the watermelon. Add the peaches, strawberries, lemon or lime juice, basil, and crushed ice and stir well.

*   Ladle into serving bowls or glasses, and serve.

FRUIT & NUT BARS

Ingredients

200 g (1 cup) pitted dates
150 g (1½ cups) rolled oats
150 g (1 cup) pecans, chopped
60 g (½ cup) macadamia nuts, chopped
60 g (⅓ cup) each dried papaya, cherries & blue-

berries, coarsely chopped
2 tbsp oat bran
3 tbsp ground flaxseed
2 tbsp wheatgerm
¼ tsp sea salt flakes
½ tsp ground cinnamon
3 tbsp honey

Special Tip:

These fruit bars are packed with nutrients and energy-giving ingredients. They also contain quite a few calories so don't eat more than one a day.

Method:

355 CALORIES

* Preheat the oven to 180°C (350°F/gas 4). Butter a 23-cm (9-inch) square baking pan.

* Place the dates in a small saucepan, cover with cold water, and bring to a gentle simmer. Drain well and chop in a food processor until smooth.

* Combine the oats, pecans, macadamias, papaya, cherries, blueberries, oat bran, flaxseed, wheatgerm, salt, and cinnamon in a large bowl. Mix in the dates and honey.

* Press the mixture into the prepared pan in an even layer.

* Bake for 20–25 minutes, until firm and golden brown. Cool completely in the pan. Cut into bars and serve.

ALMOND CAKE

SERVES: 10

Ingredients

4 large free-range eggs
2 tbsp finely grated unwaxed lemon zest
½ tsp ground cinnamon
¼ tsp ground cardamom
100 g (½ cup) brown sugar
175 g (1¾ cups) finely ground

almond meal
1 tsp baking powder
¼ tsp salt
1 tsp white wine vinegar
4 tbsp slivered almonds
Confectioners' (icing) sugar, to dust

Special Tip:

This is an old Italian recipe. Save it for special occasions.

Method:

200 CALORIES

* Preheat the oven to 180°C (350°F/gas 4). Grease a 23-cm (9-inch) springform pan and line with parchment paper.

* Beat the egg yolks, lemon zest and 50 g (¼ cup) of sugar in a bowl until pale and creamy.

* Beat the almond meal, cinnamon, cardamom, and baking powder into the egg yolk mixture with a wooden spoon.

* Beat the egg whites in a bowl with an electric mixer. When bubbles start to

form, add the salt and vinegar and beat on medium. Gradually add the remaining sugar. Beat until soft peaks form.

* Fold the egg whites into the almond mixture one large spoonful at a time.

* Spoon the batter into the prepared pan. Sprinkle with the slivered almonds. Bake for 30–40 minutes, until golden.

* Let cool on a wire rack for 15 minutes, then transfer to a serving. Dust with the confectioners' sugar, slice, and serve.

OATMEAL COOKIES

MAKES: 24

Ingredients

150 g (1 cup) plain (all-purpose) flour
1 tsp baking powder
½ tsp sea salt flakes
½ tsp ground cinnamon
75 g (⅓ cup) firmly packed dark brown sugar

180 ml (¾ cup) unsweetened applesauce
100 g (1 cup) rolled oats
60 g (½ cup) dried cranberries
60 g (½ cup) chopped walnuts

Special Tip:

These chewy little cookies can be served for dessert but are also good at breakfast or brunch, or anytime during the day when you need a healthy boost of energy.

Method:

80 CALORIES

* Preheat the oven to 180°C (350°F/gas 4). Oil two large baking sheets.

* Combine the flour, baking powder, salt, and cinnamon in a bowl.

* Beat the brown sugar, white sugar, and applesauce in a bowl until well combined. Stir in the flour mixture, then add the rolled oats, cranberries, and walnuts, stirring until combined.

* Drop rounded teaspoonfuls of the dough onto the prepared baking sheets, spacing about 5 cm (2 inches) apart.

* Bake for 10–12 minutes, until golden brown. Let the cookies cool and harden slightly on the baking sheets, 2–3 minutes.

* Transfer to a wire rack and let cool completely.

CHOCOLATE MOUSSE

SERVES: 4

Ingredients

100 g (3½ oz) dark chocolate
(70% cocoa), chopped
1 tbsp unsweetened cocoa
powder
½ tsp coffee granules
½ tsp vanilla essence (extract)

2 tbsp boiling water
2 large free-range egg whites
1 tbsp superfine (caster) sugar
120 ml (½ cup) plain Greek
yoghurt
Fresh raspberries, to decorate

Special Tip:

The really good news is that dark chocolate is good for your heath.
It is also quite high in calories, so keep it for a special treat.

Method:

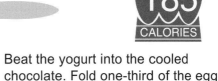

185 CALORIES

*   Put the chocolate in the top of a double boiler. Mix the cocoa, coffee, and vanilla with the boiling water, and add to the chocolate. Stir over barely simmering water until melted. Set aside to cool slightly.

*   Beat the egg whites in a bowl until soft peaks form, then beat in the sugar until thick and glossy.

*   Beat the yogurt into the cooled chocolate. Fold one-third of the egg whites into the chocolate mixture, then fold in the remaining whites.

*   Spoon the chocolate mixture into four serving cups or glasses and chill for at least 4 hours, or overnight.

*   Sprinkle with the raspberries just before serving.